# OLD PLANTATION DAYS

# OLD PLANTATION DAYS

## BEING RECOLLECTIONS OF SOUTHERN LIFE BEFORE THE CIVIL WAR

BY
MRS. N. B. DE SAUSSURE

KALPAZ

ISBN: 978-93-5128-685-1(HB)

First Published in 1909
Indian Reprint in 2017

*Published by*

Kalpaz Publications
C-30, Satyawati Nagar,
Delhi – 110052
E-mail: kalpaz@hotmail.com
Website: kalpazpublications.com
Ph.: +91-9212142040

## AUTHOR'S NOTE

THE following reminiscences are published at the request of many friends who, after reading the manuscript, have urged that the recollections be given more permanent form and a wider circulation.

N. B. DESAUSSURE.

# Old Plantation Days

MY DEAR GRANDDAUGHTER DOROTHY:

Grandmother is growing to be an old lady, and as you are still too young to remember all she has told you of her own and your mother's people, she is going to write down her recollections that you may thus gain a true knowledge of the old plantation days, now forever gone, from one whose life was spent amid those scenes.

The South as I knew it has disappeared; the New South has risen from its ashes, filled with the energetic spirit of a new age. You can only know the New South, but there is a generation, now passing away, which holds in loving memory the South as it used to be.

Those memories are a legacy to the new generation from the old, and it behooves the old to hand them down to the new.

"The days that are no more" come crowding around me, insistent that I interpret them as I knew them; there are the happy plantation days, the recollection of which causes my heart to throb again with youthful pleasure, and near them are the days, the dreadful days, of war and fire and famine. I shrink as the memory of these draws near.

The spirit of those early days is what I chiefly desire to leave with you; the bare facts are history, but just as the days come back to my recollection I will write about them, and necessarily the record will be fitful memories woven together but imperfectly.

My father, your great-grandfather, was a direct descendant on his mother's side of Landgrave Smith, first Colonial Governor of

South Carolina, his mother being Landgrave Smith's granddaughter; his grandfather was Pierre Robert, a Huguenot minister who emigrated to America, after the revocation of the edict of Nantes, and led the Huguenot colony to South Carolina.

My father was born in 1791 in the old homestead situated forty miles up the river from Savannah. He had twelve children, and I was one of the younger members of his large family. His early life was similar to the life of any present-day boy, with school days and holidays. During the holidays he enjoyed the excellent hunting and fishing which our large plantation afforded and which gave him great skill in those sports; later in life he brought up his own sons to enjoy them with him. He used to tell us, to our great entertainment, many incidents of his childhood days. When a little boy he used to drive through the country with his grandmother in a coach and four.

After he left South Carolina College he made a trip through the North on horseback, as this was before the time of railroads. It took him a month to reach Pennsylvania and New York State, and as it was in the year of 1812, he happened to ride out of Baltimore as the British rode in.

We children were always delighted when father told us of his many adventures, and the strange sights he saw during his travels. One episode always greatly shocked us, which was that of his seeing men in the public bakeries in Pennsylvania mixing bread dough with their bare feet.

After father returned home he married a cousin, Miss Robert. He had one son by this marriage, at whose birth the young mother died. This son returning from a Northern college on the first steamboat ever run between Charleston and New York, was drowned; for the vessel foundered and was lost off the coast of North Carolina.

Father's second wife was a descendant of the Mays of Virginia, who were descendants of the Earl of Stafford's younger brother. This lady was my own dear mother and your great-grandmother.

I must now tell you something about *her* grandmother, for my mother inherited much of her wonderful character from this stalwart Revolutionary character. My great-grandmother's eldest son, at nineteen, was a captain in the Revolutionary War, and she was left alone, a widow on her plantation. When the British made a raid on her home, carrying off everything, she remained undaunted, and, mounting a horse, rode in hot haste to where the army was stationed, and asked to see the general in command. Her persistence gained admittance. She stated her case and the condition in which the British soldiers had left her home, and pleaded her cause with so much eloquence that the general ordered the spoils returned to her.

Dearest child, in the intrepid spirit of this ancestor you will find the keynote to the brave spirit of the women of the South.

This old lady, who was your great-great-great-grandmother, lived to be a hundred and six years old; her skin was like parchment and very wrinkled; she died at last from an accident. I have heard my mother say that she was a remarkable character, never idle, and her mind perfectly clear until the day of her death. At her advanced age she knitted socks for my eldest brother, a baby then, thus always finding something useful to employ her mind and her hands.

Her son, my mother's father, was one of the most generous and benevolent of men, a pioneer of Methodism in that section of the country. He had a room in his house called "the minister's room." The ministers who went from place to place preaching were called circuit riders. These ministers always stayed at his house, hence "the minister's room" was very seldom vacant, and some ministers lived with him always.

Once there was a great scarcity of corn caused by a drought. Grandfather came to the rescue of the neighborhood. He sent a raft down to Savannah, which was the nearest town, and had brought back, at his expense, two thousand bushels of corn. He then sent out word to the poor of the surrounding country to come to him for what corn they needed, making each applicant give him a note for what he received. When he had thus provided for the immediate wants of the people, he generously tore up the notes; for he had only taken them to prevent fraud.

You will naturally wish me to tell you something of my mother, your great-grandmother. She was born on March 25, 1801, and was educated at the Moravian School in North Carolina, which is still in existence. I saw a very interesting description of this school in the *Tribune* of March, 1904.

Mother was well educated in all branches taught during her girlhood. Even after she was seventy-five years old she could repeat every rule of grammar and she always wrote with ease and correctness. This shows that what was taught in those days was taught with thoroughness, even if the studies were few and simple compared to the intricate and manifold ones of the present day. Mother was a woman of remarkable sweetness of disposition and intelligence, and had great executive ability, which latter quality was indispensable in the mistress of a large household of children and servants. She gave unceasing care and attention to her children, and personally supervised every detail of their education. Besides these duties, the negroes of the plantation, their food and clothing, care of their infants and the sick, all came under her control.

My father and mother inherited most of their negroes, and there was an attachment existing between master and mistress and their slaves which one who had never borne such a relation could never understand.

"Uncle Tom's Cabin" has set the standard in the North, and it seems useless for those who owned and loved the negroes to say there was any other method used in their management than that of strictest severity;

but let me tell you that in one of my rare visits South to my own people, the old-time darkies, our former slaves, walked twenty miles to see "Miss Nancy" and her little daughter, and the latter, your dear mother, would often be surprised, when taken impulsively in their big black arms, and hugged and kissed and cried over "for ol' times' sake."

When I would inquire into their welfare and present condition I heard but one refrain, "I'd never known what it was to suffer till freedom came, and we lost our master." Yes, Dorothy dear, a lot of children unprepared to enjoy the Emancipation Proclamation were suddenly confronted with life's problems.

I have beside me a letter from a friend, now in South Africa. She says in part: "I am sure you, too, would have thought much on the many problems presented by this black people. It is perfectly appalling when one thinks that they are really human beings! Human beings without any humanity, and not the slightest suggestion that there is any vital spark on which to begin work, for apparently they have no affection for anybody or anything, and it is an insult to a good dog to compare them to animals."

Such, my dear child, is the African in his native country at the present day, the twentieth century, and such was the imported African before he was Christianized and humanized by the people of the South. In order to show you that I am not prejudiced in favor of the Southerners' treatment of their slaves I will insert a letter from Dr. Edward Lathrop, whose daughter was an old schoolmate of mine at Miss Bonney's in Philadelphia.

JULY 23, 1903.

MY DEAR MRS. DE SAUSSURE:

I will proceed to answer your inquiries. You know I am Southern born and raised. I am a Georgian, and although never a slaveholder I was nursed by a negro woman to whom I was most fondly attached, and who, I believe, loved me as she would her own son. I have had the opportunity to mingle freely with slaveholders of different characters and dispositions, and while I regard slavery as such an enormous evil and am heartily glad that it has been abolished in this country, I am bound in candor to say that my observation, during all these years of my residence in Georgia and South Carolina, thoroughly convinced me that in the majority of cases slaves were more kindly treated and brought into more intimate and kindly relations to white families than they are now, though free. This, of course, is not given as an apology for slavery, but it is a simple statement of facts. I might refer, for example, to what I witnessed and *felt*, while a guest, on more than one occasion, in the house of your honored father and mother. Your father seemed to me to be as watchful of the interests, both temporal and spiritual, of his slaves as of his own immediate white family. It was, to my mind, a beautiful illustration of patriarchal slavery, as it existed in the days of Abraham. Of course there were exceptions to this treatment of slaves by their owners, but, as a rule, so far as my observation extended, your father's methods were universally approved, while the cruel slaveholder was indignantly condemned and repudiated.

You may remember that I was for three years the associate of Rev. Dr. Fuller, then pastor of the Baptist Church in Beaufort, S. C.

Beaufort District (now county) was probably the largest slaveholding district in the State.

Most that I have stated above, as to the kindly treatment of slaves was emphatically true of Beaufort. The Baptist Church, in addition to its white membership, embraced about two thousand slaves. These slaves, as church members, enjoyed equal privileges with the whites. Dr. Fuller or myself preached to them every Sunday. The Lord's Supper was administered to them and to the whites impartially and at the same time. And any grievance that they complained of, among themselves, was as patiently listened to and adjusted as was the case with the white members. In a word, all that could be done for them, in their circumstances, was promptly and cheerfully done. I could add much more of the same tenor to what I have written, but I will not weary you with a long discourse.

Affectionately yours,
EDWARD LATHROP.

To this let me add this editorial from the New York *Sun* of February 1, 1907, bearing on the question.

"UNCLE REMUS ON THE NEGRO

"We see no occasion for the astonishment that has been aroused in this part of the country by the eloquent and touching tribute to the negro's virtues by Mr. Joel Chandler Harris, of Georgia. It is by no means the first time he has spoken to the same effect, nor is he the only Southerner of his class who has proclaimed similar opinions. It ought to be perfectly well known to the entire country that the better class of whites dwell in peace and kindness and good will with their colored fellow-creatures, and that practically all of the so-called 'race conflicts' are the product of an ancient hate dating back far beyond the Civil War and involving, now as always hitherto, no one of whom either race is at all proud.

"This is a flagrant truth which Northern people have had the opportunity of assimilating any time during the past forty years. The emancipation of the slaves, effected in reality after the surrender of Lee, Johnson and Kirby Smith, made no change in the purely personal relations between the freedmen and their former masters. Not even the abominable episode of reconstruction availed to eradicate the affectionate entente of the classes and turn them against each other to the evil ends of animosity and vengeance. The old slaveholders knew that their quondam servants and dependents were innocent of vicious purpose. The latter understood full well that when in need of help and sympathy and pitying ministrations the former offered them their only sure refuge and relief. No actor in this mournful tragedy has forgotten anything. No political or social transmutation has changed anything so far as these two are concerned. The quarrels and the violent and bloody clashes of which so much is made in our newspapers, whether through honest ignorance or malign intent, are far outside of the philosophy of any important element of the Southern population.

"Joel Chandler Harris tells the simple truth when he says that the negroes of the South are moving onward, accumulating property, making themselves useful citizens and cementing the hallowed ties of respect and confidence between the classes which represent the South's righteousness and civilization. In this section we concern ourselves too much with the insignificant minority. We accept the testimony of the 'educated' few on the negro side—educated to little more than a fruitless smattering of vanity and conceit—and we much too easily imagine that the Southern 'cracker' stands for the ideas and illustrates the methods of the whites. No falser or more misleading hypothesis could be presented. The negro who typifies violence and barbarism is one in ten thousand. The white man who employs the shotgun and the torch is quite as unimportant. We shower our solicitudes on the pestiferous exception and overlook the wholesome rule.

"Uncle Remus knows what he is talking about—knows it to its deepest depth."

I think if I were to give you an account of one day as spent by my mother, it would best present an idea of the arduous duties of an old-time Southern lady on a plantation. My mother had a magnificent constitution or she could never have accomplished the amount of work required of her. I never knew her to have until her latter years a physician for herself. But for family needs we had colored nurses who, under a physician, were competent and devoted in sickness.

The day was always begun with family prayers, for my father's religious principles were his staff in life, and he derived much strength from them. His devotion to Christ was unusual, and I never knew him to doubt for an instant that he himself was a child of God. Having a most affectionate disposition, he loved his wife and children intensely, and lived in and for them. Fortunately, the love he gave them was fully returned, and I doubt if there was ever a more devoted and united family.

At sunset it was a sacred custom of his to go into a room in a wing of the house, removed from all noise, and kneel in prayer. Every child and grandchild would follow him to the quiet room, and as we knelt by his side, he would commend us to God's loving care, and rise from his knees to kiss each one of us, sons and daughters alike. No matter what our occupation or pleasures were, we would hasten home that we might not miss this sunset prayer, for then all differences that had grown up between us in the day would be healed, and we felt ourselves drawn into one united family again. My brothers and sisters, old men and women now, can never speak of that sacred hour without tears.

I will here copy a letter received not long

ago from a dear friend, Miss Morse, for years one of the faculty of Vassar College, that you may see how our home life affected "strangers within our gates."

My Precious Friend:

In asking me to give you my recollections of that cultivated consecrated home where I spent a delightful half year, you have given me a privilege. I love to recall that period, so unique in my experience.

Your father had arranged for my journey. A son came from Princeton to go with me to the steamer, and at Savannah his factor placed me in your father's boat, going up the river by night, to his plantation home.

This was my first acquaintance with negroes. At first I was afraid, being the only white person on board, but as I remembered that it was your father's plan, I knew it must be safe, and gave myself up to the enjoyment of the scene. A happier set of beings than the negroes on board it would be hard to find.

The night was dark, but on deck they gathered in groups about their bright fires, roasting corn and singing their quaint and wonderfully sweet plantation songs.

At daybreak we reached your father's landing, where you were waiting for me in the carriage, and when we drove up to the beautiful home, there were your parents at the door, ready to give me a truly Southern welcome.

Breakfast was served, and as your father asked the blessing, he prayed most earnestly that old Maum Mary might be found that day; every day the prayer was repeated, till he felt she could not be living, and then it was changed to a request that they might find her body to give it burial. She was an old negress, who had lost her mind, and, fearing she might stray away and get lost, your father had placed her daughter-in-law, a bright young negress, in the house with her, to care for her and specially to watch, lest in her mental weakness she might stray away; what he feared happened, for the daughter-in-law proved less tender and faithful than the master, and the old woman escaped.

When all hope of finding her alive was gone, the prayer of the master was that they might find her body and give it burial, but even this was not granted him.

It was a revelation to me of the tender care that old patriarch gave to his slaves, no wonder that they loved him.

You used to ask me, almost daily, to go with you to see some feeble old woman, who might be lonely and would be looking for you to come and see her, and I could hardly help shrinking as you would allow yourself to be gathered into her arms, and the petting would be mutual.

If a negro was sick, your father would always send him food from his own table, which was received with great pleasure.

At the time I was there your mother had become too feeble to continue her daily rounds among the sick and feeble, taking medicine, looking after bandages on broken limbs, etc., but an older daughter had taken her place to some extent.

I enjoyed very much the prayer-meeting evenings of the negroes. The Methodists had one evening and the Baptists another. They always held them in a building especially made for that purpose, and the singing, as it came through our open windows, was very sweet. Your father had to limit the time or they would have continued the services all night.

On Sunday they attended the same churches as the family, the galleries being reserved for them. I might have added in telling of their prayer meeting, that when we were present they always prayed for "Ole Massa and Missus," and the various members of the family, including the "young Missus from the North."

The little negro children would leave their play to gather around me as they saw me walking about the grounds.

As I recall a day in that home, so filled with love and peace, I think of the morning and evening prayers where the dear old patriarch seemed to be talking to a friend whom he trusted and loved.

Every morning his horse was brought to the door for him to ride over the plantation.

His daughter Nannie never failed to be there to help him on with his coat, and at his return to take off his wraps, bring him his dressing-gown, and cover him as he lay down to rest.

In fact, from morning till night she seemed always to have him in her thoughts, to anticipate every wish, and give him most devoted attention. I am sure it must always be a sweet memory to her that she never overlooked a possible opportunity of adding to his happiness. Few fathers receive such devoted attention from their children.

Do you remember how I used to enjoy the blaze of the pine knots in the fireplace in your room at night, and how, as they burned out, you would say to Susan, your maid, "Now throw on another knot for Miss Morse?" And do you remember how I used to ride about alone on your pet horse?

Oh, what a happy winter that was! The whole atmosphere was one of love—love between parents and children, and love that overflowed till it seemed to me that every negro on the place must feel the effects of it. Certainly every sick or aged one received tenderest care.

I remember your mother, in telling me of her heavy duties in caring for so large a family, mentioned an instance in which she had to go every day to dress a broken arm of a negro child, because the mother was too indolent to attend to it.

On Sundays your mother and her daughters used to go around to the negroes' houses to read the Bible, and teach the children Bible verses.

I hope that the reading of these memories

will recall to you something of the sweetness of that dear home, consecrated by your parents' prayers.

Lovingly,

Your "MORSIE."

This has been a long digression from the one day in my mother's life I promised to depict for you, but those early scenes come into my mind so fast that the letter from my dear friend telling of them seemed most appropriately to come into the story just at that point. But to return—after breakfast it was customary for the head nurse to report any cases of sickness on the plantation to my mother. Mother's medicine chest was brought out and together they consulted about the condition of each patient. If anyone were very ill, a man was sent to call in a physician who lived several miles away.

My mother then hastened to the negro quarters, and if the invalids could be removed they were brought to the sick house—a large, long building fitted with cots—where they could be better cared for.

One of my earliest recollections was to follow mother with my brothers and sisters, each child carrying a plate filled with food from the table for the convalescents, and, although at this day contagious diseases are so carefully avoided, I can remember going fearlessly in and out of the cabins, carrying dainty dishes to many little ones who were suffering with what they then called putrid sore throat. It was really diphtheria, and, strange to say, not one of our family took the disease, though there were forty cases on the plantation. They were taken to the pine land, so that the good air might aid their recovery.

After attending the sick, mother's next duty was to give out the daily provisions. She made a pretty picture in her quaint gown carrying a basket of keys on her arm. The Bible verse, "She looketh well to the ways of her household, and eateth not the bread of idleness," could well have been written of her. With twenty-five house and garden servants and the many little children to be looked after, this daily provisioning took a great deal of time, and thought.

The house servants had their own kitchen and cook. The negro children were under the care of a woman in a building apart, in fact, it was like a modern day nursery, where the working mothers could leave their children in safety. The older children about the place helped in the care of the little ones. Mothers with babies were only required to do light work, such as raking leaves, spinning, or sewing, that they might be ready and in condition to nurse their babies.

I can remember going to this nursery with mother frequently, for she always wanted to know that the children's food was properly prepared. They had vegetable soups with corn meal " dodgers " or dumplings, of which they were very fond. Sometimes corn bread in place of these, and as much hominy and sweet potatoes as they wanted.

Father had hundreds of cattle, cows, sheep, and hogs. We milked sixty cows on the plantation, and all the milk which had been set and skimmed was given to the negroes who came to the dairy to carry it to their homes in great tubs, and the little ones trotted along carrying their " piggins," which was the name for their small wooden buckets. The milk which had turned to clabber, " bonny clabber " as the Scotch call it, was considered a most delightful dish in our hot climate. It is so refreshing when cold that you often see me eating it now for tea.

Mother's vegetable gardens were then visited. These gardens were noted; they were so unusual in their beautiful arrangement that all strangers who came to the neighborhood were brought to see them. The walks were graveled and rolled, and myriads of bright flowers formed borders for the beds.

The poultry yards required supervision and care and were kept in perfect order. There were many acres, so-called "runs," planted in rye and other grains, for the use of the poultry, where they roved at will with some one to follow and bring them back to the yards at night, to be locked up. I often used to hear mother say "five hundred chickens, one hundred geese, one hundred turkeys, and one hundred ducks, were necessary to be kept on hand for table use."

Another care of hers was to provide clothing for all the negroes, of whom there were over five hundred. To accomplish this, seamstresses were at work all the year round; three in the house and five or six in the negro quarters. These made the men's and women's clothing. All the cutting was done under mother's supervision; and during the early part of the war, all the spinning and weaving of cloth, and even of blankets, was done on the plantation. At one time I remember seeing two thousand yards of cloth ready to make up into clothes. Fifteen years after the war, on my visit South, I saw the negro women still wearing some of the dresses which were woven at that time. The cloth went by the name of "homespun." I am giving you a rather minute account, because I want you, my darling, to gain as intimate a knowledge as possible of that life which has forever passed away.

I remember seeing my mother come into the house from her morning rounds, tired, but cheered with the consciousness that no duty had been neglected.

You will wonder how she found any time to give to her children; but we were busy in school all those hours. We had a schoolhouse on the plantation where we went after breakfast with our governess. In those days, as teachers were not paid well for their services, it was difficult to find refined and cultured people to fill the position. Knowing this, father paid the highest salaries and thus secured the best talent there was to be had for us. One of our teachers afterwards opened a school in Philadelphia, and another held an important position at Vassar College.

Besides a governess, we also had a music teacher, so we were expected to devote many hours to practicing music, and thus we were employed while mother was busy housekeeping.

The governesses were always astonished at the wonderful energy and ability shown by my mother in managing her household. I have heard them say that if Northern people could only view a Southern woman's daily life, how impressed they would be.

As soon as the girls in our family were old enough they were sent North to school to finish their education, and the boys were sent to Northern colleges.

I went for a time to a boarding school near Columbia, at the early age of twelve, and at fifteen went North with my sister, your great-aunt Catherine Robert. Father objected to my leaving home again, as he wanted me near him, but mother said education was all important, and the personal sacrifice had to be made. In my seventeenth year, I again went North with three brothers and a sister, thus making five of us studying at Princeton and at Philadelphia.

My parents were left alone, and out of their brood of twelve not one remained in the home nest, as six elder ones had married, and one other was dead. Father said he missed us so terribly that he felt as if he could not live without one of us with him. I returned, therefore, and remained with my parents until I was married. This long residence at home will account for my knowledge of everything concerning the dear father and mother, who were so devoted to their children.

Right here, speaking of my boarding-school days at Columbia, I must tell you about my pet deer. It is another digression, dear child, but I would like you to know about the pet I thought so much of, and who so dearly loved me.

Our plantation was, and still is, famed for game of all kinds, particularly deer. For many miles there were hunting grounds, now owned by Northern men, who have learned how full of game that section of South Carolina is.

As a child I was especially fond of pets, and knowing this, my friends often gave me birds, or animals, to which I was very devoted. One day there came to me in this way a young fawn, which had been caught by negroes. So young was this gentle little creature that I had to feed it from a bottle. I spent most of my time with it out of doors, and it became very much attached to me. My mother was always very particular about the complexion of her children, as most

Southern little girls are apt to become much freckled by the hot sun. So we were all obliged to wear sunbonnets, and I can see this little deer now running along beside me, with the sunbonnet I should have been wearing tied on its head.

As the fawn grew older it still remained so gentle that it would go into the house with me and follow me upstairs and lie down by the bed. As the autumn approached and the evenings grew cold, it would come into the house and lie down before the open fire just as a dog would do. Our dogs never disturbed it by day, but we were afraid to trust them at night, so Willie, for that was my pet's name, was always locked up in a little house we had for her. When she was three months old I went to boarding school, and was gone nine months. It nearly broke my heart to leave Willie, but my father, and in fact, everyone promised to take good care of her, and let nothing happen to her. Regularly I heard from her through them until near the time for my return, when the home letter ceased to speak of her.

I looked forward to my home-coming with great delight, and my first question when I arrived was concerning Willie. It was then I learned that she had gone to the swamps and had frequently been seen with other deer. Occasionally she had revisited her adopted home, so they told me, coming in and out past the dogs, not seeming to be at all afraid of them. My father suggested that I should go with him into the fields where she had been most frequently seen feeding with a number of deer, and see if we could obtain a glimpse of her.

Mounted on our favorite horses, we started off and rode through the open country. We had gone but a couple of miles when my father pointed in the distance to a group of his negroes, who were working in a field, saying that Willie was likely to be found near them, for he had seen her, at intervals, feeding with other deer in that vicinity. He noticed then that she would leave her companions, and approach the negroes, but would not allow them to touch her. We stopped our horses and looked around over the lovely country. Suddenly my father exclaimed, "Look, Nannie, look!" pointing toward the west. Standing before the setting sun, their graceful forms clearly outlined, were five or six deer.

We approached cautiously, not wishing to frighten them. At last I dismounted and as I ventured nearer, I saw the deer lift up their startled heads, and heard the faint tinkle of Willie's bell; for I had placed a heavy leather strap with a bell around her neck, to protect her against the hunters, as no one would knowingly kill a pet deer.

Father cried out to me, " Call her by name, as you used to do." I called, " Willie, Willie." At the sound of my voice the beautiful little creature lifted her head and stood still and listened, while the other deer fled; then evidently impelled by recollection, she bounded toward me. I wish I could picture the scene to you, Dorothy, and do justice to it. If anyone has ever seen a deer in full motion, he could never forget it. She came bounding toward me over the high furrows, her feet scarcely touching the ground. I ran forward to meet her, and threw my arms around her neck. The joy she manifested amazed my father. She rubbed her face all over my face and neck, and tried to show me in every way her delight in being with me again. I remained in the field petting her until nearly dark, when my father urged the necessity of our returning home. I bade her farewell for I had no thought that she would follow me, but after mounting my horse, she trotted along by my side just as a dog would do. At the entrance to our place was a high fence with eleven bars. As my father opened the gate for me to pass through, he quickly shut it against Willie, saying he wanted to see what she would do with such a barrier between us. Nothing daunted she immediately bounded over the fence, which was a remarkable jump for any animal, and followed us up to the house. When I dismounted she followed me into the yard, passing fearlessly among the hunting dogs.

She remained at home with me as long as my vacation lasted, and became as docile and gentle as she was before, not making any effort to return to her wild life. After my vacation was over and I returned to school, she went back to the woods and spent the winter there. In the spring on my return, I was frequently told by the hunters that they had seen her with her fawns. She was known throughout the entire section, and being belled all could avoid shooting her.

One day I was driving to church and saw her on the edge of the deep woods with her two beautiful fawns. I ordered the driver to stop quickly, and jumped out of the carriage, running toward her and calling her by her name. She stood as if she remembered my voice, but her fawns fled in terror and she went bounding after them. That was the last time I ever saw her for she died of black tongue. A hunter found her in the woods, unstrapped her bell and brought it to me, and I kept it for years, until in the war it was lost with everything else.

But to return to the plantation life. This life has been written of by many authors, and "Southern hospitality" is proverbial, so you will not be surprised at my description of our way of living. English people who visited us said it was like the English country life. We kept "open house"; everybody was welcome, and our many horses were at the disposal of the guest. My father's stables held thirty horses, many of them work animals, of course, but among them were fine saddle horses, always ready for the use of our friends.

Often our stables were emptied of their occupants to make room for "company horses," that is, those brought by our friends when they came to visit us.

Near our house there was a two-story building built for the accommodation of gentlemen, strangers. As there were no inns in our country, and plantations were miles apart, some provision had to be made for the entertainment of travelers, who were never turned away. We often had delightful house parties and hunting parties, but our chief enjoyment was riding through the wild and beautiful country. We also went on fishing excursions, and on picnics. We thought nothing of driving ten miles to dine at a neighbor's house.

Gentlemen visiting, brought their valets and dogs for hunting, and young ladies came with their own maids. It was a delightful open-hearted, open-handed way of living, my child, but it was brought to an abrupt end, as you will hear.

Fortunately my mother had a fine housekeeper who relieved her of the care of the culinary department. This housekeeper was famed as a cook, and her table is still remembered by everyone who sat around it.

Perhaps it would be interesting just here to explain how we came to have so competent a person in the house. During my father's early married life preparations were made to build a church in the neighborhood, (Robertville) called after the family. A contractor was engaged from the North to build the church. He brought workmen with him, and among them was a carpenter belonging to a better class of Irish than was usually found in such a trade. He brought his wife and three children with him, and during the summer contracted a violent fever. Father always thought it his duty to visit all the sick in the neighborhood; therefore, he saw him frequently, caring for his needs. When the poor man found that he could not live, he asked my father to provide for his wife and children, which my father consented to do. He kept his promise, and after the husband's death, took the three little ones home with their mother, and made them comfortable in one of the many outbuildings always found on a Southern plantation. In a few weeks the mother gave birth to a little girl and died, leaving the four little orphans in my father's care. Father wished to adopt them all, but my mother, with her usual good judgment, said she was willing to have the care of them, but would not consent to adopting them, as she did not think it well to have children of another nationality brought up as our sisters and brothers.

Eventually three of these little people were adopted by those who had no children, and one remained with us. This little girl, Margian Kane, was sent to school, but when old enough to go into higher studies refused further schooling, to learn the art of housekeeping from my mother. She died only two years ago, living to be eighty-four years old. Our family took care of her until her death. She was devoted to my father, and always remembered him with gratitude.

I love to linger over those happy, free-from-care days when our hospitable door, always open, brought so many interesting people among us, but I must push on to graver matters.

I devoted much of my time to music, especially to the harp which was my favorite instrument. Although I had several masters in music during the years I was at home, I often went to Charleston to take extra lessons. While in Charleston I met your grandfather, Henry William De Saussure, who was a descendant of the Huguenot family of that name, and a grandson of Chancellor Henry William De Saussure.

We were married at home in 1859. I have been fortunate in procuring a copy of the wedding article which appeared in the Charleston paper, the *Mercury*, 1859, which is still on file in the library there. The copy is as follows:

"On the 4th inst. at Robertville church, Beaufort District, by the Rev. J. M. Bostick, Dr. H. W. De Saussure, Jr., to Miss Nannie W., daughter of B. R. Bostick, Esq.

## For *THE MERCURY*

### The Wedding Breakfast

The Daylight Scene. The Marriage Ceremony. The Surprise. The Parting.

"The bright stars had not all disappeared on the morning of the 4th inst., when the sexton of the Robertville church commenced opening the same. The early hour, the studied neatness of his dress, and his hurried manner, all indicated that something unusual was about to occur. He had not yet completed his work, when carriages and buggies in quick succession were rapidly driven up to the church from various directions. The sun had just risen in unusual splendor as if more fully to witness the vows that were appointed to be taken at his appearing, and the company scarcely collected, when your fortunate townsman —— led to the altar Miss ——. By the altar was seated a young man, who like themselves, had just entered the threshold of life. His countenance, however, would induce the belief that he was accustomed to serious reflection. And one from his appearance pronounced him a minister. He rises, his voice falters not, but betokens a deep and heartfelt emotion, and how could it be otherwise, for he is joining in holy wedlock his sister, the playmate of his childhood hours—the object in later years of his tender solicitude and prayers. And really did it seem that he would have given worlds to insure for that couple the happiness he so devoutly implored of Heaven.

"But the marriage ceremony is ended, congratulations of friends over; and again start out a number of the happy company with the bride and groom.

"The village is left but a short distance, when our road gradually descended into a wood too damp for cultivation, but so fertile as to grow huge live oak trees, which formed with their boughs, well-nigh a continuous arch over us, from which, in most beautiful clusters almost, but not quite in one's reach, hung the wild grapes of our forest, and as the young and merry people would unsuccessfully snatch at these beautiful bunches as they rapidly passed, we were reminded of how swiftly they would pass through life, and at how many pleasures they would vainly grasp. The fifth mile is accomplished and we are on the banks of the Savannah. We had hardly time to admire the beautiful stream, when turning to the right, imagine our surprise at seeing a beautifully spread table. Curiosity soon carried us to the spot, and our astonishment was only increased when we saw the preparations that had been made.

"We soon learned that a lady who had once graced the society of Washington, and afterwards by her intelligence and accomplished manners, had delighted the society of Columbia, had sent on fishermen and cooks, and had spread this repast in honor of the new married couple, which no one would have dreamed could have been got up at such a place.

"But the breakfast is over; the dew sparkling in the grass at our feet; the happy chirp of the birds as they, too, make their morning meal on the berries and insects around us, together with the mocking birds seated in the tree above our table and seemingly conscious of their powers, have come to pay their sweet tribute to the bride, all constrain us to linger. That sister too, next to the bride in years, she feels it wrong, but yet she cannot be willing to relinquish her sister to her newly made brother. Well does she remember, how on repeated occasions, that soft voice has comforted her, and she cannot trust herself to say adieu. And little Frank has lifted his blue eyes to his mother as if to inquire, 'Will that man take away my aunty?' That look has reached his mother's heart, it is too full to explain; and she stoops to kiss away the tears from his cheeks. That brother, he is much her senior in years, he is no stranger to life's conflicts, see how his heart trembles when he says 'God bless you Nannie.'

"But the iron horse tarries on his way for none, the railroad is to be reached by such an hour and into the waiting boat step the bride and groom, the young minister and his mother. Scarcely had the boat left the shore when the oft-repeated charge is reiterated by that venerable mother to her children on shore, 'My children, take good care of your father.'

"It has not been with her one short morning of married life. Forty years ago she stood at the altar with her husband, and with him has she shared life's sorrows and joys; and for him with woman's constancy her heart still beats truest. But adieu, young and happy couple. That your boat, as it crosses the waters of life, may guide you as smoothly as it now does across the beautiful waters of the Savannah, is the sincere wish of V. . . . August 10, 1859."

Such, my dear Dorothy, is the account of my wedding which took place so many years ago, and with it ends the first period of my life.

My husband was a physician and as we were obliged, on account of his profession, to live in a central place, my father built us a lovely home in Robertville, which we occupied about three months before the war began. We moved there on December 21, 1860. Your precious mother was born March 1, 1861.

It was a turbulent time; the feeling ran

high between the North and the South, and we heard rumors of war, but it seemed too far away to invade our peaceful country.

When your mother was five weeks old we took her to Charleston to show her to your grandfather's parents—an important visit, as she was the first grand-baby in the family and they were eager to see her.

It was an all-day journey with a drive of twenty miles to the railway. We reached Charleston about eight o'clock in the evening. My father-in-law met us, and after a warm greeting to the little stranger and ourselves, said, "You are just in time to see the fight at Fort Sumter, for it begins to-night." I was terrified and begged to be taken home, but there was no train until morning and, therefore, we had to remain.

That night I was too frightened to sleep. Toward morning, about four o'clock, the first gun was fired, and it seemed to me as if it were in my room. I sprang up, as I suppose everyone else did in the city. I hurriedly dressed myself and went down to cousin Louis De Saussure's house, which is still standing on the corner of South and East Battery.

From its numerous piazzas, which commanded a fine view of the harbor, we watched every gun fired from the two forts, Moultrie and Sumter. The house was crowded with excited mothers and wives, who had sons and husbands in the fight, and every hour added to their distress and excitement, as reports, which afterwards proved false, were brought to them of wounded dear ones. It was a day I can never forget.

That night we returned to Grandfather De Saussure's and when morning came we spent another most anxious day following an anxious night, but when Fort Sumter took fire and the white flag was raised, our spirits rose over the Southern victory, to confidence and hope.

We little realized the long years of struggle that were to follow ending in defeat, and ruined homes and country. Later on I was in Charleston several times when it was under shot and shell and heard the explosions of the shells as they shrieked over our houses. Those were sad and exciting times, the awful memories of which are still active with me.

After a visit of several weeks, we returned to our home in Robertville, and my husband continued his practice, but his restlessness and anxiety to join the army was so great that I ceased to dissuade him. Physicians were needed at home, but he thought the older men should serve there, and the younger go to the front. He joined the Charleston Light

Dragoons, and became surgeon of Major Trenholm's brigade. When this brigade was was transferred to Virginia, he was, on account of his health, detailed to look after the hospitals on the coast.

But before we left our home, the fort below our country town, Beaufort, was taken, and the Northern fleet sailed in while the inhabitants were asleep. This fight at Port Royal was the second battle of the war.

When the tidings of the invasions of their town was brought to them, the people, thinking the town would be shelled, fled in their carriages, many of them not waiting to dress themselves, so great was their fright. This long procession of carriages and wagons passed through our village about dusk, the occupants not knowing what to do or where to go. Every house was thrown open to them and these first refugees remained in the neighborhood during the war. They were taken care of, until in turn we had to flee before Sherman's army.

When Dr. De Saussure went into service I returned to my father's home and lived there until Sherman drove us out. I made many visits to my husband while he was in camp. I would load a wagon with provisions, and take my trusted butler, who was a good cook and equal to any emergency, and so we would arrive on the scene of action.

We lived in a cabin of two rooms not more than twelve by fifteen feet, for whenever my husband was stationed at any special hospital he would tell the convalescent patients that if they would put up a little log cabin he would send for me. The officers would have their tents stationed around our little cabin and we had some pleasant times, though many anxious ones, for we never knew when we would be obliged to flee. Thus I experienced the pleasures and terrors of camp life. Your great-aunt Agnes, whom you met at the South as an old lady, was then a young lady visiting us. She was a beautiful girl with a voice like a bird. She was a great favorite with the officers and married Colonel Colcock, who was acting brigadier general of the coast. The time for her wedding was appointed and invitations sent out for a country wedding. The day came, and hour after hour we heard heavy cannonading. We knew a battle was being fought near us, but could learn no particulars. Evening came, and the wedding guests assembled, but no groom arrived. There was great uneasiness among the guests, and I persuaded Agnes to change her gown and come downstairs to see if her presence would not cheer the party. Although filled with anxiety herself, she followed my persuasion and behaved most admirably, but we had the wedding feast served as soon as possible, and the guests quickly departed. Everyone was anxious, and at two o'clock in the morning we heard the galloping of horses beneath the windows and a soldier called to us that he had some dispatches for us.

It proved as we thought; there had been fighting all day and Colonel Colcock was not wounded, but would come as soon as possible. Two days afterwards he appeared in the morning and brought a minister with him. He and Agnes were married at once, and he took his bride away with him; not to the camp, but to a place where she would be more comfortable, and he could sometimes see her. Their bridal trip was spent within fortifications along the coast.

Those were days of constant excitement

and unrest, as you can well imagine. Husbands and sons were all away, giving their lives in defense of their " hearth fires." The trusted negroes were our only protection and they took every care of us.

I well remember a scene that occurred about this time of the war. My youngest brother was a prisoner near Old Point Comfort, and finally received his liberty through the kindness of a fellow Southern soldier. They had been in prison six months together suffering all the hardships of prison life during war. Many times starvation stared them in the face, and upon some of the prisoners the death penalty was inflicted when the men playing together would accidentally slip over the so-called "death line." My brother was only about nineteen and the Benjamin of our family. The soldier with him had consumption and could live only a short time.

He came to my brother and said he was going to be released because they knew he would soon die. He then offered to change clothes with my brother and take his place and name, thus letting my brother go free while he remained in prison.

I heard one day cries of joy and great excitement among the negroes; hurrying to the back piazza I saw about fifty darkies, men and women crowded together bearing my brother on their shoulders, "Massa Luther, Massa's youngest boy, God bless him, God bless him," they shouted.

You can imagine the scene. We hastened down to join in the jubilation, but father and mother could scarcely get near their son, as the servants had taken complete possession of him.

When they finally made way for the master and mistress, my parents found that my brother's condition was such that he could not come into the house; he was covered with vermin. He was taken to an outhouse where he bathed, and his clothing was burned. Then he told us of his many adventures and his hard time in prison, where he would indeed have starved had it not been for kind friends at the North, who sent him money which enabled him to buy food, and he told us of the great sacrifice the Southern soldier had made for him. My father immediately forwarded a check for a thousand dollars to the poor family whose husband and father never returned to them.

Another war incident in our family was that connected with a brother's son. At the early age of fifteen, he ran away to go into the Southern army. His mother could not make him return, so she called a young colored man, who was a devoted servant of the family, to her and said to him, "John, go with your young master, and whatever happens to him, bring him back to me, wounded or dead, bring him back to me."

This young man's bravery made him known throughout the regiment. He was finally wounded, and died in North Carolina in a hospital, John never leaving him. After his death, John put him in a pine coffin roughly knocked together and started home with him. In the month of August the devoted servant reached his mistress, having been two weeks on the way. He would tell his story and beg for help to take his young master home, according to his promise to his mistress.

In spite of many misrepresentations by those who can never comprehend the tender attachment existing in those days between master and slave, I want you to have a clear idea of it, and I want you to know that the Southerner understood, and understands to this day, the negro's character better than the Northerner, and is in the main kinder to, and more forbearing with him. There were countless incidents during the war of love and loyalty shown by the negroes to their former owners, which you will read of in the many stories written now by those who know the truth.

The year 1864, in the month of December, found me still in the old homestead.

Sherman had passed on the Georgia side of the river, to Savannah, which was taken. We wondered what would be his next move, but never for an instant thought he would retrace his steps, and go through South Carolina.

The Southern troops which had guarded Savannah retreated to our neighborhood, and we cared for them for several weeks. There were at least five thousand troops on our plantation of nine thousand acres. Barbecues of whole beeves, hogs, and sheep were ordered for them. The officers were fed in the house, there being sometimes two hundred a day. The soldiers had their meals in camp.

All planters in South Carolina were restricted by law in planting cotton. Only three acres were allowed to the negro worker, thus causing a large amount of corn and other such grain to be raised, because the Confederate Government wanted this to provide for the Southern army.

Thousands of bushels of corn could not be housed, but were harvested and left in pens in the fields. Father had ten thousand bushels of corn on our plantation.

We did not sell cotton during the war. For

money we had no use, as everything was grown or manufactured on the plantation. We had a steam mill for sawing lumber, and mills for grinding corn and wheat. Sugar was made in quantities for negroes, but there was no way of refining it.

Everything was bountiful and we lacked nothing, but coffee and tea. Every known and unknown substitute was used for these drinks, but none were satisfactory; otherwise we never lived with greater abundance.

Our swamps yielded us all game bountifully, venison, wild turkeys, partridges, and reed birds. It was a rich country and could feed an army.

I met and conversed with many of the chief officers, and consulted them about the advisability of sending my father, who was then seventy years of age, away from his home.

The officers urged us to do so, as they feared the Northern army would invade our State and township. So very reluctantly father and mother left their loved home, which they were destined never to see again. They went to live with a married daughter, who had a home in an adjoining county. Some of their negroes pleaded to go with them, and about fifty followed with wagons filled with their effects.

It was a wise provision that father was spared the sight of the destruction of his house and property, and possibly personal violence from the hands of the Northern soldiers, for during the raid, my uncle, an old man who was reputed to be wealthy was asked by the soldiers where he had buried his gold; and twice was he hung by them and cut down when unconscious, because he would not confess its hiding place. My child, he had no gold, his wealth lay in his land and negroes.

Shortly after father and mother's departure, one morning, early, the remaining negroes came running to the house in a state of wild excitement, and said that Sherman's army was crossing the Savannah River at the next landing below my father's. I was picking oranges when the news came. Green oranges, blossoms, and ripe fruit all hung together on the tree. It was a favorite tree grown to an unusual size by the care given it, as it was always protected in winter. I have only to close my eyes at any time and see plainly the beautiful tree in all its glory of fruit and flower. We had picked from it that day a thousand oranges, the most luscious fruit, but they were left for Sherman's army to devour, for we were thrown into a panic by the news the negroes brought us, and hastily got into our carriages and fled. The negroes followed us in wagons, and we left our lovely home as if we had gone for a drive.

Our flight has always reminded me of Jacob's going down into Egypt, a caravan of people, for as we fled we first took with us our dear father and mother, then as the panic spread, one married daughter with all her children joined us, and then another, until we finally numbered about forty persons journeying northward. In order that you may understand how our numbers increased so rapidly, I must tell you that father gave each of his children at marriage a plantation with negroes and a house. These homes were in an adjoining county, that of Barnwell, and as we passed through this county different members of the family would join us.

On the second day of our journey your

mother was taken with a sore throat and high fever, and as we had no bed to lay her on we took turns in holding her in our arms. Thus we traveled to the upper part of the State fleeing from the army of invaders at whose hands we expected no mercy of any kind.

An old school friend of mine, Georgiana Dargan, daughter of the Chancellor of South Carolina, had written me repeatedly during the war to come to her. She had never married and lived in a large Southern colonial mansion situated on a beautiful estate. We, in our need, thought of her and pushed on, hoping she could receive us all. We were not disappointed, the house was thrown open to us and we received a warm welcome.

It was a strange fate that Sherman followed us in our flight passing through Columbia and within ten miles of us. His scouts came in and stole all our horses, except a few which we had time to hide in the swamps. The soldiers ordered many of the negroes, choosing the best young men, to mount the horses and go with them. All of them returned to us that night; they had broken away from camp, but were on foot. But let me tell you here, Sherman's army burned Columbia. He denied it, but we know he did it for my husband's sister, Mrs. Thomas Clarkson, who lived there, was ill, and the soldiers lifted her out of bed and laid her in the street while the torch was put to her home. Then, too, only three years ago, the burning of Columbia was admitted to me by a Northern general, General Howard. These were his words: "Sherman did not burn Columbia, but I am sorry to say his troops did." They got hold of liquor and so became mercilessly destructive. Sherman may not have given the order, but he was undoubtedly responsible for the plunder and destruction engaged in by those under his command. The people of Columbia were left without shelter or food, " Only women and children to wage war against," as a venerable judge, Judge William De Saussure, an uncle of Dr. De Saussure, told Sherman in pleading for clemency.

We were about fifty miles above Columbia, and as the army passed us they went on to Cheraw, a town lying on the northern border of South Carolina, forty miles above us.

There your great-grandfather De Saussure, who was an old man, had fled from his home in Charleston with his five daughters. In a few days news was brought us that Cheraw had been burned, and everybody was starving.

I was naturally eager to go to the assistance of my husband's people, and I went to one of my sisters-in-law asking her if she would be willing to accompany me to Cheraw, a drive of forty miles. She said she would go with me. Joe, my butler, to whom I was very much attached, agreed to drive us. We borrowed a pair of mules and started in the early morning with corn meal and bacon and flour for my husband's people. We had driven only a few miles when we came to the road passed over by Sherman only four days before. Such sights as we beheld along that road; dead horses, disemboweled cattle, dead dogs, and as it was in spring they were all decomposed because of our hot climate. At every turn of the road we expected to meet outriders from the Northern army. It was a day of great fatigue and fear. Our mules were lazy and would not move out of a walk.

Joe mounted one of them, and strove in vain to urge them on faster.

The day seemed endless to us, but the hours wore on, and the sun was just setting as we crawled up a final hill, when we were startled by seeing a number of men on horseback approaching, who we were sure were soldiers. My heart sank, for I expected our carriage would be confiscated as well as the mules, and we left to spend the night unprotected in the woods.

As the horsemen drew nearer, I saw to my joy that there was a mixture of blue and gray uniforms. The men were evidently of our army, for Southerners often wore at this stage of the war any kind of clothing they could get hold of to cover them. One of the officers rode up to us, and to my great surprise and delight, I found he was Major Colcock, whom I well knew, as he was a brother of Colonel Colcock, sister Agnes's husband.

Our surprise was mutual. He exclaimed, " Why Mrs. De Saussure, what are you doing here? " I replied, " Trying to reach Cheraw to take provisions in to the aid of my husband's father and sisters."

" To Cheraw," he exclaimed, " a most difficult journey, madam; the roads are in a dreadful condition and the little flat boat that crosses the river is in such demand I doubt if you can get it."

" I will not turn back, Major Colcock," I replied. " I must go on." So we parted, he going his way and I mine.

After two hours of weary travel, we reached the river and were fortunate in finding the boat could carry us over the river. We crossed and reached the town of Cheraw at ten o'clock at night. A scene of desolation greeted my eyes the next morning; all the public buildings had been burned, houses alone were standing amid desolate surroundings. The De Saussure family and others had been living on scorched rice and corn, scraped from the ashes. Officers as well as soldiers had gone into houses and taken all food that could be found and burned it in the yards of the various houses; leaving the women and children to starve. My beautiful harp, which after cutting the strings, I had sent to Cheraw for safety in care of Mr. De Saussure, had narrowly escaped being taken by some officers. They asked to have the box opened for them, but Mr. De Saussure told them the harp was out of order, so they passed it by. My harp was safe, but your great-aunt Agnes was not so fortunate with her piano. It was a gift from her father when she left school, and a beautiful Steinway. When she married Colonel Colcock, he said to her: " Ship your piano to Charleston; it will be safer there than in the country." Colonel Colcock was from Charleston and had relatives to whom he wrote asking them to care for the piano, when it arrived. It reached Charleston just about the time the city fell into the hands of the enemy. Colonel Colcock's uncle went down to the station to get it, when he learned that an officer had taken it and shipped it off to the North.

Twenty years after the war, this notice published in the *News and Courier* of Charleston was sent me from different parts of the South:

## NOTICE

### A RELIC OF THE WAR

Miss Nannie Bostick's Music Book in the Hands of a Federal Soldier.

To the editor of the *News and Courier*: Will you insert the following in your paper, as it will be of benefit to one of South Carolina's ladies:

If Miss Nannie Bostick will communicate with Captain James B. Rife, Middletown, Dauphin County, Pennsylvania, she will learn something to her advantage.

I have in my possession a music book which was captured or stolen by some one during the war, and I would like to return it to her if she still lives. By so doing you will greatly oblige,

Yours very truly, JAS. B. RIFE,
Late Capt. U. S. A.

MIDDLETOWN, DAUPHIN COUNTY, PA.,
January 26, 1889.

The Miss Nannie Bostick above referred to afterwards married Dr. Henry De Saussure, of this city. After his death she was for a long time employed as an instructor at Vassar College, N. Y., and is now a resident of Brooklyn. The home of Colonel Bostick, the father of Mrs. De Saussure, on Black Swamp, in Beaufort (now Hampton) County, was burned by General Sherman's army in the grand "march to the sea."

On reading it I was of course, much excited and wrote immediately to the gentleman in Meadsville, telling him I was the person he was looking for. I waited three weeks most anxiously, and then received a letter from his sister saying that for years her brother had been trying to find me, and that he had something to tell me which was communicated to him by a dying soldier. The sister further wrote that her brother had advertised in New York and Southern papers before, and the cause of his doing so again was that a young niece visiting them, in looking over some old books had come across a music book with my name on it. She went with it into his room, and said, "Uncle, who is Miss Nannie, W. Bostick?"

He sprang from his chair exclaiming, "What do you know about her?"

When he learned that she knew nothing and had merely seen my name on the old music book, he said, "I will try once more to find her," and sent off the notice to the *News and Courier* of Charleston.

As fate would have it the next day, on his way to Harrisburg to make arrangements for a Cleveland procession, his horse took fright from a trolley car, and in the accident he was instantly killed.

The music book was returned to me by his

sister, but whatever the secret was that he had carried so many years, it died with him, for no one else knew it.

After his death his sister asked me to visit her. She said my name was so often on her brother's lips, and she only knew he wanted to communicate something of importance, but what it was he had never told her. He was a prominent man in the army. She sent me his photograph and the notice of his death.

You can imagine this incident brought back many memories. What could have been the dying soldier's communication that Captain Rife wished so much to tell me, and which he never intrusted to any other member of his family? And where had this very heavy, old music book, in his possession, been found? My sisters, when I met them, talked the matter over with me, and Agnes said: "I remember putting a lot of books, among them some of yours, with my piano to pack it tightly." When it was shipped North the book was found with the piano, as I have since ascertained.

We wondered that the music book had ever come back to me, its rightful owner, but since I have lived at the North, even family Bibles, which were taken from the old homes, have been returned to me. Looting was the order of the day during the Civil War, and wanton destruction followed.

I once went South with old Captain Berry, who for twenty years had charge of a steamer plying between Charleston and New York. Your mamma and myself were the only ladies on board, as the time was in July when the tide of travel was northward. The officers of the steamer were exceedingly kind to us, and told us many interesting stories of their seafaring lives.

Captain Berry told me of a trip he made from New Orleans to New York, when General Ben Butler was there in command. A division of the army was being transferred and Captain Berry said that besides soldiers the vessel was laden with all kinds of handsome furniture, with pictures, pianos, and trunks filled with women's clothing, from a lady's bonnet to slippers. That division of the army which Captain Berry was bringing North belonged to one of the generals under Butler's command.

The vessel was laden, the last soldier had stepped aboard, when just before the gangplank was lowered, a jet-black pony was hurried aboard, a perfect beauty. Then a lady was seen rapidly riding along the wharf; she quickly jumped from her horse, and went on board inquiring for the general; when he was pointed out to her she stepped up to him and said: " General ——, you have taken my husband's last gift to his little boy, the pony; I have come to ask you to return him to me." The general turned a deaf ear to her request, and as he did so, she drew her whip across his face with a stinging lash. Had he lifted his finger to her in return, Captain Berry said, the soldiers would have shot him dead.

During that trip North in the silence of the night, the soldiers went down into the hold of the vessel, opened every box, cut strings on pianos, ruined pictures and other things with ashes and water, then nailed up every box carefully and put it in place again. This was done by the Northern soldiers on board who knew of and resented the wrong done to the people of New Orleans. The poor little pony never reached his destination, for he was found dead the next morning; a mysterious death, but the soldiers knew, and had had a hand in his taking off. Thus they avenged the lady to whom their sympathy had gone out.

Captain Berry was a Northern man, but his frequent visits to Charleston had thrown him into intimate relations with the Southern people and he admired them greatly.

We spent six months, from December, 1864, until June, 1865, at Darlington, our place of retreat. It was a hard winter; food was scarce, and little but the coarsest kind could be bought.

By spring we had grown hopeless, and well I remember that while walking in the garden some one called out to me, "The war is over, Lee has surrendered." My feelings were tumultuous; joy and sorrow strove with each other. Joy in the hope of having my husband and the brothers and friends who were left, return to me, but oh, such sorrow over our defeat!

In the course of time, the men of our family returned with the exception of your great-uncle Edward, my brother, who had gone through the war, but was finally killed in the last two weeks of fighting around Petersburg, Va.

As one after another of the family came back to us, worn out and dispirited, our thoughts turned to the dear old home on the Savannah River, and we longed to go back. Before yielding to our desires, it was considered wise for the men of the family to go first and investigate. They found only ashes and ruin everywhere in our neighborhood, and father's place, except a few negro cabins, was burned to the ground. There were thirty buildings destroyed.

The steam mill, blacksmith's shop, carpenter's shop, barns, and house—nothing was left standing except chimney and brick walls to mark the place of our once prosperous, happy home. There was but one fence paling to indicate the site of our little village. The church, too, was burned, and now negro cabins are standing where it once graced the landscape. Our beautiful lawns were plowed up and planted in potatoes and corn by the negroes, who were told we would never return.

Sherman left a track of fire for three hundred miles through the State. When you hear the war song "Marching through Georgia," which stirs the hearts of the Northerner, think of the scenes of desolation and heartbreak the song recalls to the Southerner.

When I left my own home in Robertville,

I took the daguerreotypes of my old schoolmates, Northern girls, of whom I was fond, and opening the clasps I stood them all in a row on the mantel, hoping that should some commander find among them the face of a relative, he would spare the house for the sake of friendship. It was a vain hope, for my lovely house was destroyed with all the others. However, a soldier, brother of one of the girls, did find among the pictures the likeness of his sister and he wrote me after the war about thus seeing amid the roar of battle the likeness of his angel sister, for she was then dead.

You will often hear of the " reconstruction period," the period when the situation had to be faced by the beaten Southerner, and everything had to be managed on a new and strange basis. That period in my life had now come, for we all resolved to return home and do the best we could with what we had left.

Father had loaned the Confederate Government fifty horses and mules; twenty-five were returned to him, good, bad, and indifferent. We took the journey home by the aid of these animals, and our carriage was drawn by one large "raw-boned" horse helped by a little pony. We camped out at night, and drove all day. Sometimes we were able to get shelter for our parents. It was very rough traveling; the roads were destroyed, and trees had been cut down blocking the way. We finally reached the only house left standing near our former home, at eleven o'clock at night, after ten days of travel. This house was far off from all plantations, situated in a pine forest. It was used by our family for a summer retreat. It had large airy rooms; one measuring twenty-five feet, and one fifty feet. In this house, bereft of all its furniture, our family gathered. We found our negroes scattered and completely demoralized.

Starvation seemed imminent. The men of our family went to work to cut timber, to be shipped to Savannah on rafts. In the meantime, before we could expect any monetary return from this industry, what else could we do to better our condition? was the question we asked one another.

One of my brother's former negroes came to me and said, "I think you could make money by baking pies and bread for the colored Northern troops."

Those soldiers were quartered on my father's plantation. My dear, war was nothing compared to the horrors of that reconstruction period. For six months we never went to bed without bidding one another good-by, not expecting to be alive the next morning. We sold our jewelry, all that was left, to the soldiers, and they would come to the house, march around it with bayonets drawn, and curse us with the vilest oaths. We would gather the little ones around us, bar the door, and wait, for we knew not what.

When you are old enough, Dorothy, dear, read "The Leopard's Spots," which gives a better description of what we endured, than I ever can write.

However, we needed money to buy food with. I, therefore, set to work making bread, and any number of green-apple pies. Tom, a negro, built us a clay oven and we secured a negro's service for the baking; I got up at four o'clock in the morning, and by ten o'clock Tom was off with the pony and wagon, to sell articles for us. We had enough to live on, but no meat except bacon.

By request of every white person the Government removed the colored troops six months after the war, and sent white troops in their place.

Poor grandpa would sit all day with bowed head and say over and over, "My poor daughters, my poor daughters." We tried to appear brave and cheerful and would say in reply, "Why we can manage; do not trouble about us." But father's heart was broken and though he appeared well, he instinctively felt that his days were numbered and asked to have our former pastor called.

When the minister came, we and some neighbors gathered together in a little supply store that was "thrown up" after the war, and there we stood, or sat on the counters, during service. It was a touching scene. Your mother was a little girl of five years, and she feeling the sadness of it all, wept through the whole service. Father gathered her in his arms and tenderly wiped her tears away.

As service closed an old church member and father advanced to shake hands with each other saying simultaneously: "We shall drink no more of the fruit of the vine, until we drink in our Father's Kingdom."

It seemed in the nature of a prediction, for three days afterwards father passed peacefully away, without apparent illness.

Mother lived until her eighty-seventh year, weary, sad years for her. She lived with her children, but none were able to make her comfortable. Poverty reigned everywhere, and still exists in that once luxurious country. We thanked God that father had not to endure, for long, the sight of our want and distress. Before he died, however, we left the large house in which we first took refuge, and started housekeeping separately in outhouses or cabins in the pinelands, which were formerly used for storerooms, kitchens, laundries, etc.

We fitted up one of these cabins as comfortably as we could for father's and mother's use, and in another little house situated about three and a half miles from them, I lived a while with your mamma and Dr. De Saussure. In this little house we had to endure great hardships for many years, and led the most desolate lives.

Your precious mother was our only comfort; she was always happy. She had few books, no school, and as my husband was an invalid, he was often too ill to see her, or to be left alone. She would study her lessons and sit outside the door of his darkened room, and when I could leave him she would recite to me what she had learned.

Another time we lived in a little cabin, part of which was curtained off for the accommodation of a sister of Dr. De Saussure's and her baby. Our kitchen stove was under an open shed built against the side of the house. Heavy rain would flow over the dirt floor, and remain standing several inches deep.

At this time your mother's one delight was her pony Brownie. She would drive the cows up from the swamps, and Brownie soon learned to give them a bite on their backs when they stopped to graze.

"Jeff Davis" was also a great pet; he was a young calf we never allowed to leave the yard for fear the negroes would take him. Poor Jeff was sacrificed for food, but your mother's heart was broken for her pet, and she could not be induced to taste any portion of the meat.

Before I undertook to make pies and bread for the colored troops, and when we were very hard pressed, as I said before, I went and spent a night with my parents. My adopted sister, the housekeeper of whom I told you, called me out of the house and taking me some distance away so we could not be heard by them, said: "We have but a pint of corn meal in the house, and if I cook that for our supper I have nothing to give father and mother for breakfast." We cried together, and wondered what we could do. One of our negro men from the plantation approached me and said, "Miss Nancy" (they called me by that name, and the grandchildren of our old negroes still use it), "the steamboat has just landed at the dock, and there are lots of boxes for you." Amazed, I exclaimed, "Why, who has sent me anything?" I looked then upon all Northern friends as enemies. I had not heard from any of them in years; the war had separated us. I told the man to take a cart and hasten to the dock. He returned laden. Still in amaze I had the boxes opened, wherein we found all sorts of provisions: hams, sugar, tea, coffee, crackers, etc., etc., and better than all a letter from a gentleman, who wrote that he had read in the papers of the great distress of Southern people; he knew nothing of my condition, but judged of it by what he read of the pitiful state of others, and he wished me to draw whatever amount we needed from his agent in Savannah to relieve our necessities. To me the heavens had opened and from them came these gifts. I saw in this relief when we most needed help the kind care of our heavenly Father, who had put into the heart of this generous man to come to our assistance. We drew enough money to enable us to buy food and to begin work on our own place. With the account of my acquaintance with this gentleman my story will close.

He was an Englishman, who had settled with his family in the Bahamas. When I met him I was in my sixteenth year, and was on my way to school in Philadelphia. Agnes and three brothers were with me, one brother going to Princeton to finish his theological course, one to Lawrenceville to school, and the third to Colgate University.

On the steamer was this gentleman, taking his son to Philadelphia to school. My eldest brother became acquainted with him, and introduced him to me. It took much longer in those days to make the trip, the journey comprising three and a half to four days.

Agnes and I saw a great deal of the father, and the son was with my brother most of the time, so that when we reached Philadelphia, we felt well acquainted. Mr. Saunders, for that was the name of our new friend, said to my brother upon landing: " I shall be in Philadelphia a fortnight, or until my son becomes acquainted in the city. If you will allow me, I will be pleased to take your sisters driving with us, and show them the places of interest." Many pleasant drives we had together, and grew better acquainted each day.

At the end of his visit he came to bid us farewell, and said to me: " Miss Nannie, I have a request to make of you, will you grant it? " I replied, " If I can, I will gladly." He had often spoken of his elder son who was studying at Oxford, England, and he continued: " In two years my son will graduate, I want you to promise me that you will wait until you see him before engaging yourself to anyone." I laughingly promised him to wait the two years.

When I was seventeen years old I returned home. I had been there perhaps three years, when I went on a brief visit to a friend who lived about twenty miles away from us. My visit ended, I returned home, and as I drove up to the door, my young brother ran out to meet me and said, "Guess who is here to see you," and when I failed in guessing he said, "Mr. Saunders's son."

I then met the young gentleman, a handsome, fine young man, who brought letters of introduction from leading men in his own home, and one from his father, who wrote that he had not forgotten my promise to him, but that he had been delayed in fulfilling his desire in having us meet by his son's failing to find me.

He had lost the address of my home, and

thinking Charleston the nearest town, his son was sent there to inquire for us. The next winter he sent him to Savannah to find me, and from there the young man was directed to my father's home.

Mr. Saunders wrote that it had been his dearest wish to have me for his daughter, and he had talked so much to his son about me that he was quite willing to fall in with his father's wishes in the matter.

In the meantime I had met your grandfather, and had decided that I would marry him, or no one. My father was bitterly opposed to my marrying at all, as he did not want to part with me, and therefore, I was waiting until he gave his consent.

We made Mr. Saunders's visit as pleasant as possible, and I told him at once of my affection for your grandfather, as I did not wish to deceive him.

The young man spent some weeks with us, and upon his return home I received another letter from his father saying he could not give up his cherished hope of having me for a daughter, and as his son had fallen in love with me, he hoped I would reconsider my decision. At the same time his son wrote of his attachment, offering himself to me. But it was useless to urge me, and though I felt grateful to be looked upon with so much affection I declined the offer.

This was the beginning of a very remarkable friendship which sprang up between the father and myself.

Upon receipt of the letter expressing myself as steadfast to Dr. De Saussure, he wrote in reply asking that he might consider himself as a father, and to me and your mother, who always called him grandfather, he was like a father.

During the latter part of the war, I wrote to him asking if he would receive cotton through the blockade and arrange to send us in return many necessary things. We were without shoes, and were wearing clothes made from our gay silk dresses carded up and spun with cotton, thus woven into cloth by our own people. We then had an abundance of food, but other things were not to be bought. In reply he said: " Do not send your cotton, you will run a double risk; I will send you all you need, for I have more than enough for my family and yours."

Never dreaming we would ever be in a position where we could not repay Mr. Saunders, I wrote to him and sent a list of needed articles, pieces of linen, merino, and silk, and stockings and shoes for us all. He sent us two thousand dollars worth of goods in gold value, thus generously supplying every child and grandchild in our family with clothes.

Alas for us, the war ended disastrously, and forgetting all he had previously done for me and mine, he now sent money and provisions to aid us, which help arrived in our darkest hour.

I am glad to tell you that these debts were paid, though it took us years to do it.

Until Mr. Saunders's death, we corresponded regularly, and fifteen years after the war he came to see me at Vassar College, for after your grandfather's death, I came North with your darling mother who was fifteen years of age, and went first to Philadelphia, placing her in the same school where I had been educated, with the same principals still in charge, the Misses Bonney and Dillaye. I kept house in Philadelphia in a quiet way in two rooms, and had been there two years when I learned that the gentleman whom your grandfather had left in charge of my affairs had speculated and lost every cent I had in the world.

Immediately I tried to find some work by which I could support your mother and myself, and through one of my former teachers, Miss Morse, who was then assistant to Dr. Raymond of Vassar College, I was offered the position of assistant principal. There I remained for five years. While at Vassar your mother took up a special course at the College and graduated from the Art Department.

One day my dear old friend Mr. Saunders was announced. The last time we met, I was fifteen and he forty-five years old. This latter meeting took place twenty-five years later. It was a sad meeting for both of us. He had lost most of his property, and was comparatively poor. He took me in his arms and said; " My child, if I were able to take care of you and your daughter you would not be here one minute, for I would take you home with me and take care of you both." The last letter I received from him said: " I am nearly home and when I get there I shall watch for your coming."

## ADDENDUM

BEAUFORT, S. C., January 8, 1906.

MY DEAR AUNT NANNIE:

I fear you have by this time lost all hope of hearing from me, but I have not forgotten my promise. I am afraid, however, you will be very much disappointed, as I have so little information to give about family history, and that little is very scrappy. Our branch of the family have been criminally careless about preserving records.

While I have not what we lawyers would consider strict evidence of the fact, still I am quite satisfied from circumstances and inferences, which I shall not undertake in this letter to detail, that our family and the Northern family of Bostick were one and the same.

Our American progenitor landed in Plymouth, Mass., sometime about the middle of the seventeenth century, coming from Chester County, England, and being probably a political refugee. His wife also came with him from England. In England the family history was both ancient and distinguished, the founder landing on English soil with William the Conqueror, in whose service he was of distinguished rank, both military and social. In England he became one of the barons of the realm. The title remained for centuries in the family, and may be still in existence, and has been adorned by many distinguished representatives in the English wars especially. The original stock in Massachusetts seems to have migrated, mine northward and some gradually drifting southward. The intermediate links I cannot supply, but finally these brothers settled, two in Carolina, the youngest being our great-grandfather Richard, and one in Georgia. In Jones's history of Georgia mention is made of Captain Littlebury Bostick, a wealthy rice planter near Savannah. He, I think, was the brother, or son of the brother who settled in Georgia. Richard was the youngest of the three. The other brother, John, bought a large landed estate near Columbia on which he lived and died quite an old man. During his life he maintained the style and reputation of a man of great wealth, but at his death it was found that his affairs were financially involved. He never married, but was known as a cultured man of decidedly literary tastes, and was a leading figure in the social life of his section. His most intimate friend was General Hampton, father of the Confederate general of same name.

Richard settled in old Blackswamp, where

he married three times, the last two wives being sisters, both Roberts. The last, first married Singleton, and at his death our ancestor. By the last marriage there were no children; by the second marriage to Miss Robert, we are descended through your father Benjamin Robert Bostick; by the first marriage the other Blackswamp Bosticks are descended.

I have not a copy of the Bostick coat of arms, but the motto is "Always ready to serve," bestowed, or adopted, I presume, in recognition of their martial spirit exhibited on many great battlefields. The Robert family, of whom your grandmother was a member, settled in Sumter. The progenitor, Rev. Pierre Robert, led a colony of Huguenot refugees from France. Many other Huguenot families in the State claim descent on maternal lines from him. He seems to have been a man of wealth and ancient lineage. I have a copy of the French coat of arms.

Your mother, who was a Maner, came of no less distinguished line. They were of Welsh descent, and probably more remotely of Norman French descent, as the progenitor was Lord de Maner.

Grandma's mother was a May from an old Dutch family. The original May came to Charleston, and founded the first large importing house (tea chiefly) in copartnership with the famous Dutchman, Admiral Gillon.

I presume you know, of course, that your great-grandfather, William Maner, and his brother Samuel were both captains in the famous Marion Brigade in the Revolution. Your grandfather was a captain at eighteen years of age.

I may mention also, that grandma's mother, who was a May, was on her maternal side a daughter of an English Colonel Stafford. The English Staffords are also of ancient stock, I believe.

I am afraid the foregoing very meager account of the family connections will give you very little that you do not know already. While I have stated the main features of the family history, as I know them, the statement is very general. If you desire more of detail with reference to any individual or any part of the family history, I may be able to give you a little more, and will take pleasure in answering any inquiries on this line. I have had to write this very hastily.

With love from us all, I remain,

Affectionately,

A. McIver Bostick.

